PIRATES

Rebecca Rissman

Raintree

www.raintreepublishers.co.uk
Visit our website to find out more information about Raintree books.

To order:
☎ Phone 0845 6044371
🖨 Fax +44 (0) 1865 312263
✉ Email myorders@raintreepublishers.co.uk

Customers from outside the UK please telephone +44 1865 312262

Raintree is an imprint of Capstone Global Library Limited, a company incorporated in England and Wales having its registered office at 7 Pilgrim Street, London, EC4V 6LB – Registered company number: 6695582

Edited by Rebecca Rissman, Nancy Dickmann, and Siân Smith
Designed by Joanna Hinton Malivoire and Ryan Frieson
Original illustrations © Capstone Global Library 2010
Illustrated by Mendola Ltd
Picture research by Tracy Cummins
Production control by Victoria Fitzgerald
Originated by Capstone Global Library Ltd
Printed and bound in China by CTPS

ISBN 978 1 406216 18 9 (hardback)
14 13 12 11 10
10 9 8 7 6 5 4 3 2 1

ISBN 978 1 406216 23 3 (paperback)
15 14 13 12 11
10 9 8 7 6 5 4 3 2 1

British Library Cataloguing in Publication Data
Rissman, Rebecca
Pirates. – (Legends of the sea)
910.4'5-dc22
A full catalogue record for this book is available from the British Library.

Acknowledgements
We would like to thank the following for permission to reproduce photographs: akg-images p.9; AP Photo p.15 (J. Pat Carter); Corbis pp.17, 19 (© Richard T. Nowitz); Getty Images p.27 (Matthew Bash/U.S. Navy); istockphoto pp.11 (© FrankCangelosi), 20 (© NoDerog); National Geographic p.6 (Don Maitz); Shutterstock p.27 (© Map Resources); The Art Archive p.18 (Granger Collection); The Bridgeman Art Library International pp.12 (Embleton, Ron (1930-88) / Private Collection / © Look and Learn), 13 (American School, (18th century) / Private Collection / Peter Newark Historical Pictures), 21 (English School, (19th century) / Private Collection / Peter Newark Historical Pictures), 22 (English School / Private Collection / Peter Newark Historical Pictures), 24 (American School, (18th century) / Private Collection / Peter Newark Historical Pictures), 25 (Private Collection / Peter Newark American Pictures); The Granger Collection, New York pp.10, 23; The Kobal Collection p.7 (Walt Disney).

Every effort has been made to contact copyright holders of any material reproduced in this book. Any omissions will be rectified in subsequent printings if notice is given to the publisher.

Some words are shown in bold, **like this**. You can find out what they mean by looking in the glossary.

Contents

Is it true?. 4

Pirates. 6

Pirate life. 8

Look out – pirate attack ! 10

Pirate weapons 14

Pirate booty 16

Famous pirates 20

Pirates today 26

Naming activity 28

Glossary. 30

Find out more 31

Index 32

Is it true?

When it comes to pirates, some **legends**, or stories, seem too strange to be true. Can you guess if these legends are true or false?

All pirate ships flew a flag showing a skull and crossbones.

Blackbeard used to make people think he was on fire.

Pirates always buried their treasure.

Pirate ships weren't wild. In fact, they usually had a "Pirate **Code**", or list of rules they had to follow!

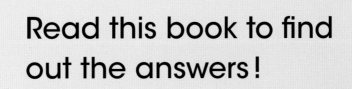

Read this book to find
out the answers!

Pirates

For as long as people have sailed the seas, there have been pirates. Pirates are sailors who attack other ships for money and power. Pirates have sailed all around the world.

This photo was taken from the film *Pirates of the Caribbean*.

Films about pirates are popular today. Film-makers find out about pirates in the past to make their films more realistic.

Pirate life

Believe it or not, a pirate's life wasn't all battles and war. Pirates spent most of their time at sea looking for their next **victims**. Life on a ship could get boring!

Pirate code

Most pirates followed a list of rules called a **code**. Some rules were:

- Lights out below **deck** at 8:00PM
- No fighting with each other
- Weapons must be kept clean and ready for use!

But when pirates spotted another ship, things could get very exciting!

Look out – *pirate attack!*

Pirates flew a flag called the Jolly Roger to warn other ships that they were going to attack. This flag scared the sailors on other boats.

Jolly Roger

IS IT TRUE?

All pirate ships flew flags showing a skull and crossbones.

11

When pirates were ready to attack, they sailed next to another ship. Then one group of pirates would tie the two boats together while another group climbed across. Once pirates boarded their **victim's** ship, the fight really started!

grappling
hook

Tools of the trade

Pirates used grappling hooks to climb onto other ships.

Pirate weapons

Once pirates boarded their **victim's** ship, they used weapons that helped them in **hand-to-hand** fighting. These included short knives and swords such as **daggers** and **cutlasses**. Pirates also used guns called **muskets** to kill their victims.

cutlass

musket

Pirates only used their cannons as a last resort. They didn't want to ruin the ships they were trying to steal!

Pirate booty

Pirates didn't attack other ships just for fun – they were after treasure! Treasure was sometimes called **booty**. Pirates also wanted to steal new ships.

treasure

real pirate treasure

DID YOU KNOW?
Pirate treasure wasn't just gold and silver. Sometimes pirates took live treasure! Holding people for **ransom** was a quick way to earn money.

Most of the time, pirates spent their treasure as fast as they could get it. But sometimes they stole so much treasure that they couldn't spend it all at once. Some pirates buried their treasure to keep it safe.

treasure

treasure

This pirate treasure was found
at the bottom of the sea.

Famous pirates

Blackbeard was one of the most famous pirates that ever lived. While he was a pirate, Blackbeard stole from more than 40 ships.

Blackbeard is so famous he has appeared on stamps!

IS IT TRUE?

To scare his **victims**, Blackbeard would light strips of cloth and tuck them into his beard. This made him look like he was on fire!

Answer: true

Black Bart

Black Bart was a very skilled pirate. **Legends** say that Black Bart stole 400 ships in just 4 years!

Another famous pirate was called Calico Jack. He was well known for his brightly coloured clothing and for allowing women to join his **crew**.

Calico Jack

Not all famous pirates were men. Two of the fiercest pirates were women. Anne Bonny and Mary Read were pirates who attacked ships and stole treasure.

Anne and Mary dressed in men's clothing. Many of their **victims** had no idea they were women!

Pirates today

There are still pirates around today. In fact, pirates rob hundreds of ships each year.

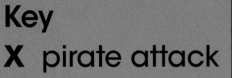

Key
X pirate attack

This map shows where the most pirate attacks occurred in 2009.

These modern pirates were captured near Somalia, in Africa.

Police and soldiers from around the world work together to keep people safe from pirates.

Naming activity

Pirates sometimes used their own words to describe things on their ships. Can you guess which word matches with each part of the picture?

Crow's nest

Figurehead

Helm

Poop deck

Answers:
1. Figurehead
2. Helm
3. Crow's nest
4. Poop deck

Glossary

booty stolen treasure. Pirate booty could include gold and jewels.

code list of rules pirates followed. Pirates followed different codes.

crew group of people who work on and run a ship

cutlass curved sword

dagger short, pointed sword similar to a knife

deck area on a boat that people could walk on. Most decks are open to the air.

grappling hook hook that pirates used to climb onto other ships

hand-to-hand close style of fighting

legend story that started long ago. Legends can be true or made up.

musket old type of gun

ransom a trade of money or other payment asked in return for a person

victim person who is tricked or harmed

Find out more

Find out

What was another name for a pirate?

Books

Horrible Histories Handbooks: Pirates, Terry Deary (Scholastic, 2006)

My Best Book of Pirates, Barnaby Harward (Kingfisher Books, 2006)

Usborne Young Reading: The Story of Pirates, Rob Lloyd Jones (Usborne Books, 2007)

Websites

www.britishcouncil.org/kids-topics-pirates.htm
Test your knowledge of pirates with the pirate quiz on this website.

www.nationalgeographic.com/pirates/index.html
Play the "high seas adventure" to find out about famous pirates, ships, treasure, and more.
Click on "Blackbeard" for the story behind this famous pirate.

www.nmm.ac.uk/explore/sea-and-ships/facts/ships-and-seafarers/pirates
This web page tells you everything you need to know about pirates.

Index

Anne Bonny 24, 25

Black Bart 22
Blackbeard 4, 20–21
booty 16–19

Calico Jack 23
cannons 15
cutlasses 14

daggers 14

famous pirates 20–25
films about pirates 7
flags 4, 10, 11

grappling hooks 13

hand-to-hand fighting
   14

Jolly Roger 10

legends 4, 22

Mary Read 24
modern pirates 26–27
muskets 14, 15

parts of a ship 28–29
Pirate code 4, 9
pirate life 8–9

ransom 17

skull and crossbones
   4, 11

treasure 4, 16–19

weapons 9, 14–15
women pirates 23,
   24–25